The Multicultural Treasury

Janina Malecka

J. Weston Walch, Publisher
Portland, Maine

This collection is intended to stimulate thinking and provoke lively discussion. Some of the entries are controversial; they have been included to represent many varying points of view. However, the quotations should not be interpreted as representing the viewpoint of the publisher.

On the cover
"Sun Owl and Foliage" by Kenojuak Ashevak, lithograph, 1979
Reproduced with permission of the West Baffin Eskimo Co-operative Ltd.,
Cape Dorset, NWT, Canada

1   2   3   4   5   6   7   8   9   10

ISBN 0-8251-2388-7

Contents

Foreword

"What, then, is the American, this new man?"

Philip Freneau, poet turned militiaman and privateer, asked this question during the American Revolution.

More than 200 years later, we need to ask, "Who are we now? Who makes up our nation?"

The Multicultural Treasury offers a way to begin exploring the answer. It is an inspired selection of more than 260 quotations, teachings, bits of folk wisdom, personal experiences, excerpts from literature, and facts. Through these revelations of pride, heart, spirit, genius, pain, and idiosyncrasies of some of the cultures most important in today's America, we can take the first steps toward understanding and appreciating the richness and diversity of our culture.

Students newly arrived from another culture will feel proud that some of their heritage is being shared with classmates. Perhaps in time they can be encouraged to share information and experiences of their own. Students whose families emigrated here years ago will have the world opened for them, with these impressive and often poignant words from other places and from histories other than their own.

For African American students, *The Multicultural Treasury* spotlights the accomplishments and stirring words of some courageous leaders. It offers samples of African thought and cultures, and presents sound advice and wise observations from outstanding contemporary African American men and women.

Native American students will see that the wise teachings of their ancient cultures are especially timely and important for today's world.

This book is divided into several sections. It begins with thoughts on a multicultural society from a wide variety of sources, then goes on to six sections, each focused on a particular cultural or geographic area.

Because of the limits of space *and* the incalculable amount and value of the experience, ideals, knowledge, and heritage of other cultures, this book is hardly even a sampler—it's more like a teaser.

Caribbean, Meso-American, and South American cultures, so important in our society, cannot be fairly represented in such a brief collection. Neither is there a fair indication of the diversity and depth of African and Asian cultures and the native cultures of the United States and Canada. There is hardly a hint of what people of these and other cultures contribute to every aspect of life here. The new leadership and participation of women from every culture cannot be fully shown. We can try to present a wider picture with further multicultural collections, but an accurate representation of these topics requires libraries of volumes.

You'll probably begin using the sections most appropriate to the backgrounds of your students. But please don't stop there.

All of the sections have important ideas that apply to all people. Yet some items that are particular to a single group can be the most effective of all. Because the quotations or experiences are so eye-opening or so stir our compassion, they might be the catalysts that start us building bridges of understanding and acceptance from person to person.

However you choose to use this book, rejoice that we have at last recognized that being made up of different cultures gives us strength and breadth and vibrance not found in melting-pot homogeneity. Offer *The Multicultural Treasury* to your students as a wonderful gift, a celebration of our diversity.

Thoughts on a Multicultural Society

As cities and states become increasingly multi-ethnic and multi-racial...what may evolve in the U.S. is a new kind of American "mainstream" defined more by shared contemporary values and less by historical roots.

—David Holmstrom

There is no they, only us.

—Bumper sticker

The politics of the next century will be triggered by increased immigration. A guideline for us may be this statement:

"Those who won our independence by revolution were not cowards. They did not fear political change. They did not exalt order at the cost of liberty."

—Louis Brandeis
Former U.S. Supreme Court Justice
Quoted by David Holmstrom

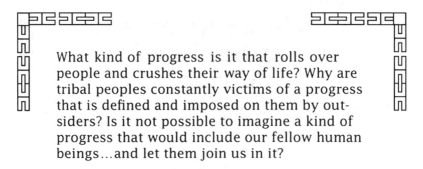

What kind of progress is it that rolls over people and crushes their way of life? Why are tribal peoples constantly victims of a progress that is defined and imposed on them by outsiders? Is it not possible to imagine a kind of progress that would include our fellow human beings...and let them join us in it?

> —*David Maybury-Lewis*
> Millenium: Tribal Wisdom
> and the Modern World *(Viking)*

Babies of all nations are alike until adults teach them.

> —*Mauree Applegate*

Can we plan a society that is not based on the domination of others and that will not end up like the chilling police paradises of the East or with the explosions of disgust and hatred that disrupt the banquet of the West?

> —*Octavio Paz*
> The Other Mexico *(Grove, 1989)*

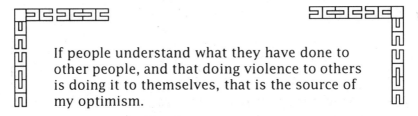

If people understand what they have done to other people, and that doing violence to others is doing it to themselves, that is the source of my optimism.

> —*Athol Fugard*
> *South African playwright*

Immigration is the sincerest form of flattery.

> —*Jack Paar*

The heart of difference between the modern world and the traditional one is that in traditional societies people are a valuable resource and the interrelations between them are carefully tended; in modern society things are valuables and people are all too often treated as disposable.

> —*David Maybury-Lewis*
> Millenium: Tribal Wisdom
> and the Modern World *(Viking)*

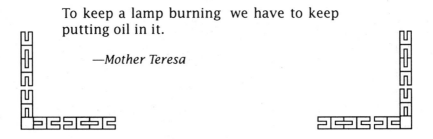

To keep a lamp burning we have to keep putting oil in it.

> —*Mother Teresa*

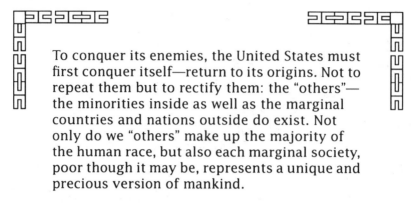

To conquer its enemies, the United States must first conquer itself—return to its origins. Not to repeat them but to rectify them: the "others"—the minorities inside as well as the marginal countries and nations outside do exist. Not only do we "others" make up the majority of the human race, but also each marginal society, poor though it may be, represents a unique and precious version of mankind.

> —*Octavio Paz*
> Mexico and the United States

We have fallen victim to a collective self-deception, a society's allowing itself to assimilate like mad from its constituent groups while representing itself to itself as if the assimilation had never happened, as if progress and good were almost exclusively Western and white.

> —*Mechal Sobel*
> The World They Made Together
> *Paraphrased by Claude M. Steele in*
> *"Race and Schooling of Black*
> *Americans" (The Atlantic Monthly)*

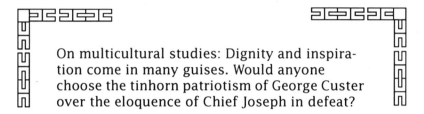

On multicultural studies: Dignity and inspiration come in many guises. Would anyone choose the tinhorn patriotism of George Custer over the eloquence of Chief Joseph in defeat?

—*Stephen Jay Gould*

Whether it's keeping the family farm, or living with ethnic diversity, history alone is no guide to the future. Solutions require movement away from the status quo. There is no way to go but forward.

—*Takashi Oka*

Native Peoples of the United States and Canada

We are entering a new era for humanity where the right to be different is being more broadly embraced—and that process is enveloping the world.

> —*Chief Ovid Mercredi*
> *Cree lawyer, Canada*

Whatever befalls the earth befalls the sons of the earth. Man did not weave the web of life, he is merely a strand in it. Whatever he does to the web, he does to himself.

> —*attributed to Chief Seattle*

Always do what you can. Learn all that's in you, and bring it out for the people to see, especially the children so they won't give up along the way.... Don't hide your talents. Bring them out of your minds for everybody to see.

> —*Essie Parrish*
> *Pomo Spiritual Leader*

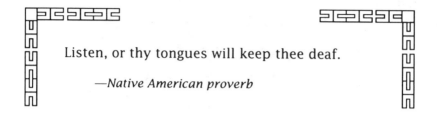

Listen, or thy tongues will keep thee deaf.

—Native American proverb

Training began with children who were taught
to sit still and enjoy it. They were taught to use
their organs of smell, to look when there was
apparently nothing to see, and to listen intern-
ally when all seemingly was quiet. A child that
cannot sit still is a half-developed child.

—Luther Standing Bear
Lakota Sioux

The true Hopi People preserve the sacred
knowledge about the way of the earth because
the true Hopi People know that the earth is a
living ... growing person ... and all things on it
are her children.

—from the Hopi Declaration of Peace

What is man without the beasts? If all the
beasts were gone, man would die from a great
loneliness of spirit. For whatever happens to
the beasts, soon happens to man. All things are
connected.

—attributed to Chief Seattle

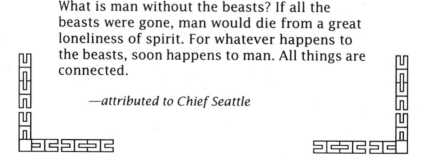

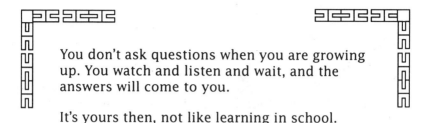

You don't ask questions when you are growing up. You watch and listen and wait, and the answers will come to you.

It's yours then, not like learning in school.

> *—Larry Bird*
> *Keres tribe*

On buying and selling land:

The idea is strange to us. If we do not own the freshness of the air, and the sparkle of the water, how can you buy them?

> *—attributed to Chief Seattle*

Beauty will come in the dawn.
And beauty will come in with the sunlight.
Beauty will come to us from everywhere,
Where the heaven ends, where the sky ends.
Beauty will surround us. We walk in beauty.

> *—Billy Yellow*
> *Navaho Medicine Man*

Native American spirituality, with its understanding of humans as part of the earth ...
teaches a certain humility and respect for life
in all its forms. Modern society['s] tendency to
see ourselves as *in charge of* rather than *part
of* life has not only polluted the environment
and oppressed our fellow man but has given
rise to ...widespread acceptance of abortion
and the growing interest in legalized euthana-
sia.

—*Claire M. Bastien*

All my life
   I have been seeking
   Seeking!

—*Death song of a Yokut Song Maker*

My children, as you travel along life's road
never harm anyone nor cause anyone to feel
sad. On the contrary, if at any time you can
make a person happy, do so.

—Winnebago elder

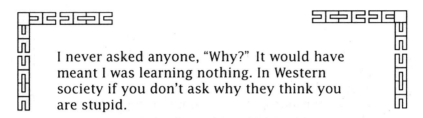

I never asked anyone, "Why?" It would have meant I was learning nothing. In Western society if you don't ask why they think you are stupid.

—Sage Track
Taos Pueblo

NEW MEXICO, 1920's

"... the Whites always want something; they are always uneasy and restless. We do not know what they want. We do not understand them. We think they are mad," said the Pueblo chief.... When psychiatrist Carl Jung asked why he thought the whites were mad, the chief said, "They say they think with their heads."

"Why, of course. What do you think with?" asked Jung.

"We think here," the chief said, indicating his heart.

—Paraphrased from On Jung
by Anthony Stevens (Penguin)

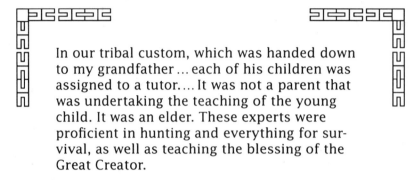

In our tribal custom, which was handed down to my grandfather... each of his children was assigned to a tutor.... It was not a parent that was undertaking the teaching of the young child. It was an elder. These experts were proficient in hunting and everything for survival, as well as teaching the blessing of the Great Creator.

      —Alex Saluskin
      Yakima

Too much thought only leads to trouble. We Eskimos do not concern ourselves with solving all riddles. We repeat the stories in the way they were told to us and with the words we ourselves remember.

      —Orulo
      Igluik Eskimo

We're growing in spirituality that was absent for some time because of the preoccupation with materialism around the world....When I say spirituality, I don't mean organized religion. I mean a sense of connectedness with the universe, with the world in general.

      —Chief Ovid Mercredi
      Cree lawyer, Canada

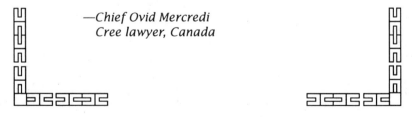

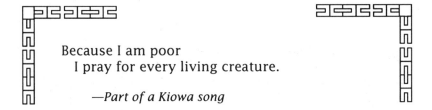

Because I am poor
  I pray for every living creature.

  —*Part of a Kiowa song*

There is no place in the white man's cities. No
place to hear the unfurling of the leaves in the
spring or the rustle of insect wings.

  —*attributed to Chief Seattle*

We were arrogant…when we colonized the
Americas. With rare exceptions…we sought
to replace the civilizations we found with
our own. As missionaries, we confused culture
and religion. We didn't build on the incredible
Franciscan-like foundation of spirituality
which was indigenous to many tribes.…
Perhaps if we had taken the time to understand
their culture and spirituality and *then* offered
ours…*we* would not have polluted the Western
hemisphere, endangering and eliminating
countless species in the process.

  —*Claire M. Bastien*

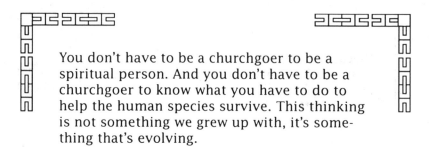

You don't have to be a churchgoer to be a spiritual person. And you don't have to be a churchgoer to know what you have to do to help the human species survive. This thinking is not something we grew up with, it's something that's evolving.

—*Chief Ovid Mercredi*
Cree lawyer, Canada

The possibility of conceiving of an individual alone in a tribal sense is ridiculous....the very complexity of tribal life and the interdependence of people on one another makes this conception improbable at best, a terrifying loss of identity at worst.

—*Vine Deloria*
Quoted in The Primal Mind:
Vision and Reality in Indian America
by Jamaka Highwater (Meridian, 1982)

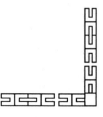

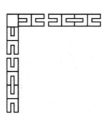
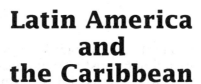

Latin America
and
the Caribbean

...We Latin Americans are uninvited guests who
have sneaked in through the West's back door,
intruders who have arrived at the feast of
modernity as the lights are about to be put out.
We arrive late everywhere, we were born when
it was already late in history, we have no past,
or, if we have one, we spit on its remains, our
peoples lay down and slept for a century and
while asleep they were robbed and now they go
about in rags...

> —*Octavio Paz*
> The Other Mexico *(Grove, 1989)*

If I asked myself, "Can the United States carry
on a dialogue with [Latin America]?", my
answer would be yes—on condition that they
first learn to speak with themselves, with their
own *otherness*: their Blacks, their Chicanos,
their young people. And something similar
must be said to Latin Americans: criticism of
others begins with criticism of oneself.

> —*Octavio Paz*
> The Other Mexico

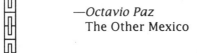

...More than 9 million indigenous people live in South America today, most of them occupying the lowest social positions and suffering from chronic poverty and racial discrimination.

"We define indigenous as those who still keep some semblance of their former culture. There are millions more who are of mixed race or who have moved away from their culture and language over the past 500 years," says Dr. [Carlos] Fuentes [coordinator general, Argentine Aboriginal Foundation].

> —*Vivek Chaudery*
> The Christian Science Monitor

The whites see only with their eyes and hear through their ears. We Indians can see and hear with our minds.

> —*Ignacio*
> *Makuna Indian of Colombia*

The land is our culture. If we were to lose this land, there would be no culture, no soul.

> —*Chief, Kuna Indians of Panama*

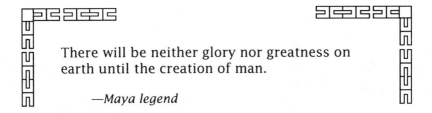

There will be neither glory nor greatness on earth until the creation of man.

—Maya legend

Their reason for killing and destroying such an infinite number of souls is that the Christians have an ultimate aim, which is to acquire gold, and to swell themselves with riches in a very brief time and thus to rise to high estate disproportionate to their merits....Those lands are so rich and felicitous, the native peoples so meek and patient, so easy to subject, that our Spaniards have no more consideration for them than beasts....But I should not say "than beasts," for, thanks be to God, they have treated beasts with some respect; I should say instead like excrement on the public squares.

—Bartolomé de Las Casas
Brief Account of the Devastation
of the Indies *(1542)*

The heart's memory eliminates the bad and magnifies the good, and...thanks to this artifice, we manage to endure the burdens of the past.

—Gabriel García Márquez
Colombian novelist
Love in the Time of Cholera *(Knopf, 1988)*

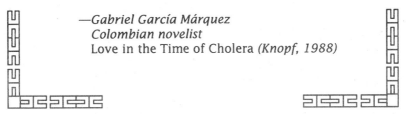

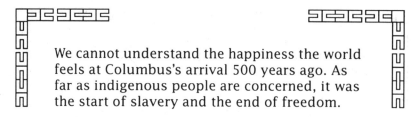

We cannot understand the happiness the world feels at Columbus's arrival 500 years ago. As far as indigenous people are concerned, it was the start of slavery and the end of freedom.

—Dr. Carlos Fuentes
Coordinator General, Argentine
Aboriginal Foundation

Habits are first cobwebs, then cables.

—Spanish proverb

What you dislike of yourself do not like for me.

—Spanish proverb

The important thing to remember is that riches...stolen from South America helped in the development of Europe and led to the underdevelopment of this continent.

—Dr. Carlos Fuentes

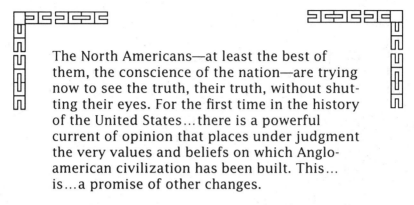

The North Americans—at least the best of them, the conscience of the nation—are trying now to see the truth, their truth, without shutting their eyes. For the first time in the history of the United States...there is a powerful current of opinion that places under judgment the very values and beliefs on which Angloamerican civilization has been built. This... is...a promise of other changes.

> —*Octavio Paz*
> The Other Mexico *(Grove, 1989)*

America means freedom. It means work. That's why we came here.

> —*Reina Ramirez Gomez*
> *Recently arrived from El Salvador*

Whoever has a tail of straw should not get too close to the fire.

> —*Latin American proverb*

The baby who doesn't cry isn't nursed.

> —*Latin American proverb*

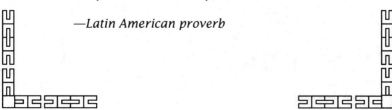

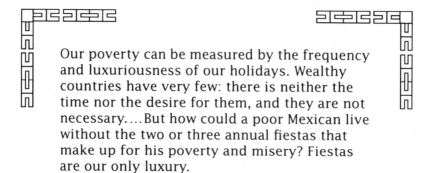

Our poverty can be measured by the frequency and luxuriousness of our holidays. Wealthy countries have very few: there is neither the time nor the desire for them, and they are not necessary....But how could a poor Mexican live without the two or three annual fiestas that make up for his poverty and misery? Fiestas are our only luxury.

—*Octavio Paz*
The Labyrinth of Solitude *(Grove, 1989)*

Envious people never compliment, they only swallow.

—*Mexican proverb*

The person who asks for little deserves nothing.

—*Mexican proverb*

Necessity is a great teacher.

—*Mexican proverb*

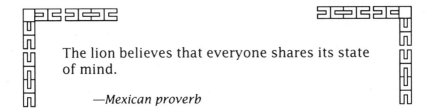

The lion believes that everyone shares its state of mind.

—*Mexican proverb*

...Perhaps the [North Americans] have never experienced true joy, which is an intoxication, a whirlwind. In the hubbub of a fiesta might our voices explode into brilliant lights, and life and death mingle together, while their vitality becomes a fixed smile that denies old age and death but that changes life into motionless stone.

—*Octavio Paz*
The Labyrinth of Solitude *(Grove, 1989)*

Everyone is the age of their heart.

—*Guatemalan proverb*

You make the road by walking on it.

—*Nicaraguan proverb*

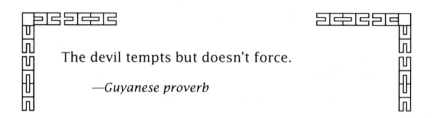

The devil tempts but doesn't force.

—Guyanese proverb

This country was guided by an instinct that can be called the wisdom of nature itself. There were no known models for its creations, and its doctrines had neither teachers nor examples, so that everything about it was original, and as pure as the inspiration that comes from on high.

—Simón Bolívar, writing of Peru

No one knows as much about the pot as the spoon does.

—Andean proverb

The continuous drip polishes the stone.

—Peruvian proverb

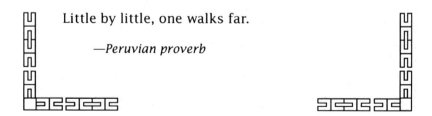

Little by little, one walks far.

—Peruvian proverb

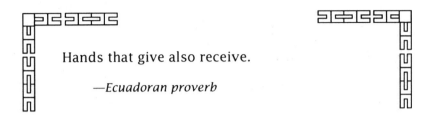

Hands that give also receive.

—*Ecuadoran proverb*

Ignorance doesn't kill you but it makes you sweat a lot.

—*Haitian proverb*

Poor people entertain with the heart.

—*Haitian proverb*

The shoe knows if the stocking has a hole.

—*Bahamian proverb*

Make a friend when you don't need one.

—*Jamaican proverb*

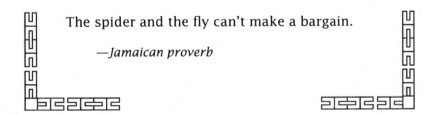

The spider and the fly can't make a bargain.

—*Jamaican proverb*

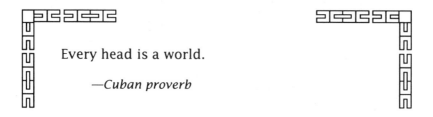

Every head is a world.

—*Cuban proverb*

...The supreme value is not the future but the present. The future is a deceitful time that always says to us, "Not yet," and thus denies us. The future is not the time of love: what a man truly wants he wants *now.* Whoever builds a house for future happiness builds a prison for the present.

—*Octavio Paz*
The Other Mexico *(Grove, 1989)*

Africa and African America

Throughout the whole of black Africa...oral chronicles had been handed down since the age of the ancient forefathers...Every living person ancestrally goes back to some time and some place where no writing existed; and then human memories and mouths and ears were the only ways those human beings could store and relay information....We who live in the western culture are so conditioned to the "crutch of print" that few among us comprehend what a trained memory is capable of.

    —*Alex Haley*
    Roots
    (Doubleday and Company, 1976)

The notion of Pan-Africanism was founded on the notion of Africa, which was, in turn, founded not on any genuine cultural commonality but...on the very European concept of the Negro....The very category of Negro is at root a European product: for the "whites" invented the Negroes in order to dominate them.

    —*Kwame Anthony Appiah*
    In My Father's House:
    Africa in the Philosophy of Culture
    (Oxford University Press, 1992)

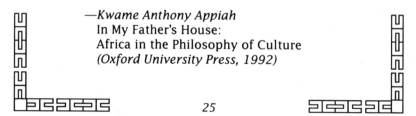

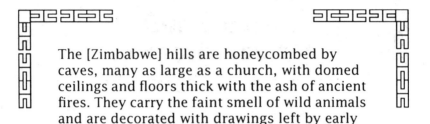

The [Zimbabwe] hills are honeycombed by caves, many as large as a church, with domed ceilings and floors thick with the ash of ancient fires. They carry the faint smell of wild animals and are decorated with drawings left by early Bushmen. These are still vivid and impressive in their accuracy, with running giraffes so perfectly realized that some drawings could be photographs.

—*Thurston Clark*

Out under the moon and the stars, alone with his son that eighth night, Omoro...lifted his baby up with his face to the heavens, and said softly, "Fend kiling dorong leh warrato ka iteh tee." ("Behold—the only thing greater than yourself.")

—*Alex Haley*
Roots
(Doubleday and Company, 1976)

It takes an entire village to raise a child.

—*African proverb*

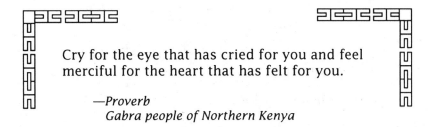

Cry for the eye that has cried for you and feel merciful for the heart that has felt for you.

—Proverb
Gabra people of Northern Kenya

Even the milk from our own animals does not belong to us. We must give it to those who need it, for the poor man shames us all.

—Gabra belief, Northern Kenya

The stars shine brightest when the moon is gone.

—Hausa (West Africa)

Abundance and scarcity are never far apart; the rich and the poor frequent the same house.

—Somali saying

One volunteer is better than ten forced men.

—African proverb

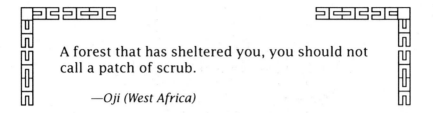

A forest that has sheltered you, you should not call a patch of scrub.

—Oji (West Africa)

Only when you have crossed the river can you say the crocodile has a lump on its snout.

—Ashanti proverb (West Africa)

If you cannot bear the smoke, you will never get to the fire.

—Wodaabe saying (West Africa)

The one being carried does not realize how far away the town is.

—Nigerian proverb

Blessed are those who can please themselves.

—Zulu saying (South Africa)

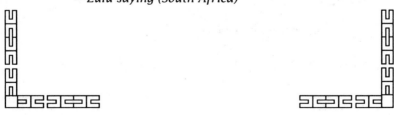

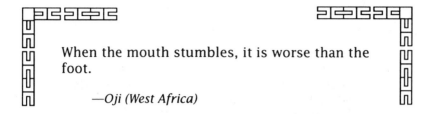

When the mouth stumbles, it is worse than the foot.

   —Oji (West Africa)

War ends nothing.

   —Zairean saying

Earth is but a marketplace; heaven is home.

   —Yoruba (West Africa)

The dream of America as the great melting pot has not been realized for the Negro; because of his skin color, he never even made it into the pot.

   —Thurgood Marshall
   U.S. Supreme Court Justice

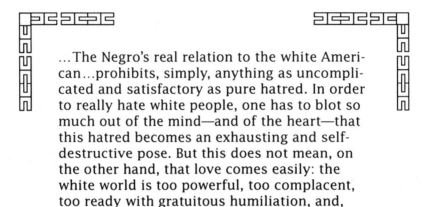

...The Negro's real relation to the white American...prohibits, simply, anything as uncomplicated and satisfactory as pure hatred. In order to really hate white people, one has to blot so much out of the mind—and of the heart—that this hatred becomes an exhausting and self-destructive pose. But this does not mean, on the other hand, that love comes easily: the white world is too powerful, too complacent, too ready with gratuitous humiliation, and, above all, too ignorant and innocent for that.

—*James Baldwin*
Notes of a Native Son *(Beacon Press, 1955)*

The experience of Negroes in America has been different in kind, not just in degree, from that of other ethnic groups. It is not merely the history of slavery alone but also that a whole people were marked as inferior by law...

—*Thurgood Marshall*
U.S. Supreme Court Justice

I am not ashamed of my grandparents having been slaves. I am only ashamed of myself for having at one time been ashamed.

—*Ralph Ellison*
Invisible Man *(Random House, 1947)*

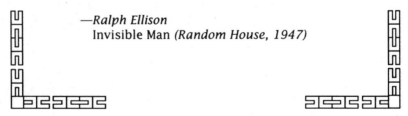

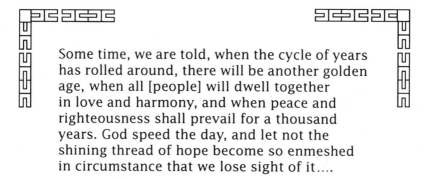

Some time, we are told, when the cycle of years
has rolled around, there will be another golden
age, when all [people] will dwell together
in love and harmony, and when peace and
righteousness shall prevail for a thousand
years. God speed the day, and let not the
shining thread of hope become so enmeshed
in circumstance that we lose sight of it....

> —*Charles Waddell Chesnutt*
> *"The Web of Circumstances"*
> *from* The Wife of His Youth and Other
> Stories of the Color Line *(1899)*

...That little man in back there, he says women
can't have as much rights as men 'cause Christ
wasn't a woman. Where did your Christ come
from? From God and a woman! Man had nothing to do with him.

> —*Sojourner Truth,*
> *former slave, addressing the*
> *Ohio Women's Rights Convention, 1851*

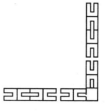

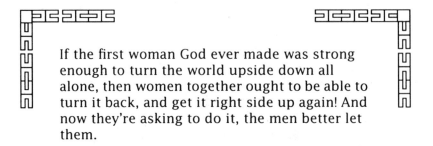

If the first woman God ever made was strong enough to turn the world upside down all alone, then women together ought to be able to turn it back, and get it right side up again! And now they're asking to do it, the men better let them.

> —*Sojourner Truth,*
> *former slave, addressing the*
> *Ohio Women's Rights Convention, 1851*

Washington entered the field to fight for the freedom of the American people—not for the white man alone, but for both black and white. Nor were they white men alone who fought for the freedom of this country. The blood of black men flowed as freely as that of white men.... And some of the very last blood shed was that of black men....

> —*John A. Copeland*
> *Free black who took part in John Brown's raid*
> *at Harper's Ferry, Virginia, 1859, in a letter*
> *to his family*

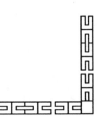

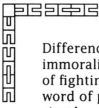

Differences made on account of ignorance,
immorality, or disease are legitimate methods
of fighting evil, and against them we have no
word of protest; but discrimination based
simply and solely on physical peculiarities,
place of birth, color of skin, are relics of that
unreasoning human savagery of which the
world is and ought to be thoroughly
ashamed....

> —*"Declaration of Principles" of the
> Niagara Movement, 1905*

[The Niagara Movement was founded by black intellectuals
from 14 states, led by W. E. B. DuBois, to end all distinc-
tions based on race.]

This is the country to which we Soldiers of
Democracy return. This is the fatherland for
which we fought! But it is our fatherland. It is
right for us to fight.... By the God of heaven, we
are cowards and jackasses if now that the war
is over, we do not marshal every ounce of our
brain and brawn to fight a sterner, longer, more
unbending battle against the forces of hell
in our land....

Make way for Democracy! We saved it in
France...and we will save it in the United States
of America, or know the reason why.

> —*W. E. B. Dubois, on
> the Black Veterans of World War I*

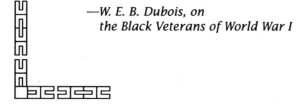
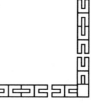

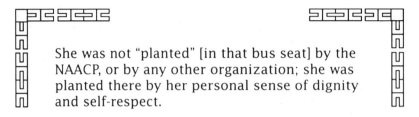

She was not "planted" [in that bus seat] by the
NAACP, or by any other organization; she was
planted there by her personal sense of dignity
and self-respect.

—Dr. Martin Luther King, Jr., on
Rosa Parks, 1955

...In spite of the difficulties and frustrations of
the moment, I still have a dream. It is a dream
deeply rooted in the American dream.

I have a dream that one day this nation will rise
up and live out the true meaning of its creed
"...that all men are created equal."

I have a dream that my four little children will
one day live in a nation where they will not be
judged by the color of their skin but by the
content of their character.

—Dr. Martin Luther King, Jr.
Washington, D.C., 1963

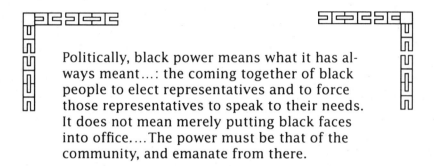

Politically, black power means what it has always meant...: the coming together of black
people to elect representatives and to force
those representatives to speak to their needs.
It does not mean merely putting black faces
into office....The power must be that of the
community, and emanate from there.

—Stokely Carmichael on Black Power
from The New York Review of Books, *1966*

The vindication of Dr. King's historic endeavors
can only come through our renewed dedication
to the human goals of brotherly love and equal
justice which he so nobly advanced.

—Senator Edward Brooke, (R) Mass.,
after the assassination of
Dr. Martin Luther King, Jr.

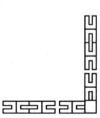

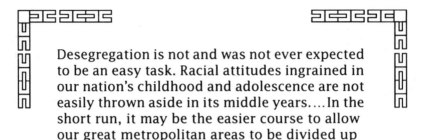

Desegregation is not and was not ever expected to be an easy task. Racial attitudes ingrained in our nation's childhood and adolescence are not easily thrown aside in its middle years....In the short run, it may be the easier course to allow our great metropolitan areas to be divided up into two cities—one white, the other black—but it is a course, I predict, our people will ultimately regret.

I dissent.

—Supreme Court Justice Thurgood Marshall's
dissent in Milliken vs. Bradley, 1974
(Supreme Court vote against ordering
desegregation across district lines)

Most poor people are not on welfare....

I know they work. I'm a witness. They catch the early bus. They work every day. They raise other people's children. They work every day. They clean the streets....They change the beds you slept in in these hotels last night and can't get a union contract. They work every day... and yet when they get sick, they cannot lie in the bed they made up every day. America, that is not right. We are a better nation than that....

—from Jesse Jackson's address to the
1984 Democratic National Convention

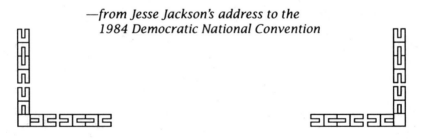

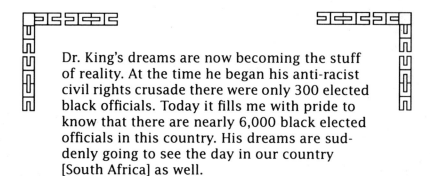

Dr. King's dreams are now becoming the stuff of reality. At the time he began his anti-racist civil rights crusade there were only 300 elected black officials. Today it fills me with pride to know that there are nearly 6,000 black elected officials in this country. His dreams are suddenly going to see the day in our country [South Africa] as well.

—from Nelson Mandela's Atlanta
address of June 27, 1990

One must seek the noblest and best in the individual life only: each soul must save itself.

—Claude McKay
Quoted in Claude McKay: A Black Poet's Struggle for Identity *by Tyrone Tillery (University of Massachusetts)*

Never hang your head down. Never give up and sit down and grieve. Find another way. And don't pray when it rains if you don't pray when the sun shines.

—Sachel Paige

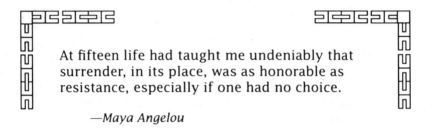

At fifteen life had taught me undeniably that
surrender, in its place, was as honorable as
resistance, especially if one had no choice.

—*Maya Angelou*

Remediation defeats, challenge strengthens.

—*Claude M. Steele*
"Race and the Schooling of Black Americans"
(The Atlantic Monthly)

There is always something left to love. And if
you ain't learned that, you ain't learned
nothing....Child, when do you think is the time
to love somebody the most? When they done
good and made things easy for everybody?
Well then, you ain't through learning—because
that ain't the time at all. It's when he's at his
lowest and can't believe in hisself 'cause the
world done whipped him so! When you starts
measuring somebody, measure him right,
child, measure him right. Make sure you done
taken into account what hills and valleys he
come through before he got to wherever he is.

—*Mama in* A Raisin in the Sun
by Lorraine Hansberry (Dutton, 1958)

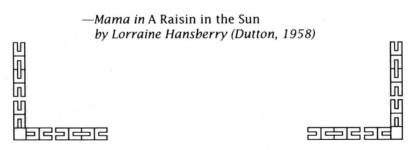

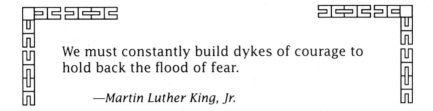

We must constantly build dykes of courage to hold back the flood of fear.

—*Martin Luther King, Jr.*

There's a period of life where we swallow a knowledge of ourselves and it becomes either good or sour inside.

—*Pearl Bailey*

As long as you keep a person down, some part of you has to be down there to hold him down, so it means you cannot soar as you otherwise might.

—*Marian Anderson*

It's time for us to turn to each other, not on each other.

—*Jesse Jackson*

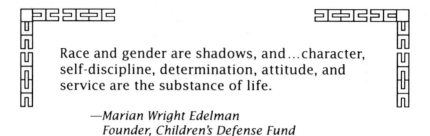

Race and gender are shadows, and...character, self-discipline, determination, attitude, and service are the substance of life.

—*Marian Wright Edelman*
Founder, Children's Defense Fund

Leadership should be born out of the understanding of the needs of those who would be affected by it.

—*Marian Anderson*

I must use the manure that has been thrown on me to fertilize myself and grow from seed again.

—*Eartha Kitt*

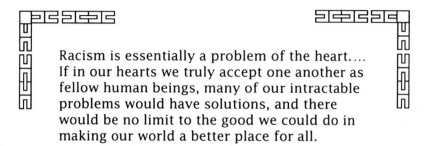

Racism is essentially a problem of the heart.... If in our hearts we truly accept one another as fellow human beings, many of our intractable problems would have solutions, and there would be no limit to the good we could do in making our world a better place for all.

—*Mark and Gail Mathabane*
Love in Black and White:
The Triumph of Love Over Prejudice
and Taboo *(HarperCollins, 1992)*

Children have never been very good at listening to their elders, but they have never failed to imitate them.

—*James Baldwin*

Sometimes it's worse to win a fight than to lose.

—*Billie Holiday*

There are ways of dealing with the world that invite energy in. You have to be excited by the things you don't know. This keeps you constantly stimulated, on a learning spree with life.

—*Diana Ross*

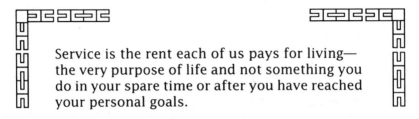

Service is the rent each of us pays for living—
the very purpose of life and not something you
do in your spare time or after you have reached
your personal goals.

—Marian Wright Edelman

I don't know the key to success, but the key to
failure is to try to please everyone.

—Bill Cosby

Health nuts are going to feel stupid some day,
lying in hospitals dying of nothing.

—Redd Foxx

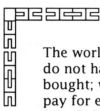

The world needs more men [and women] who do not have a price at which they can be bought; who do not borrow from integrity to pay for expediency; whose handshake is an ironclad contract; who are not afraid of risk; who are honest in small matters as they are in large ones; whose ambitions are big enough to include others; who know how to win with grace and lose with dignity; who do not believe that shrewdness and cunning and ruthlessness are the keys to success; who are not afraid to go against public opinion and do not believe in "consensus"; who are occasionally wrong and always willing to admit it. In short, the world needs leaders.

> *—Anonymous*
> *Quoted by Marian Wright Edelman in*
> The Measure of Our Success: A Letter
> to My Children and Yours *(Beacon Press)*

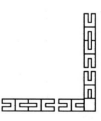

Eastern Europe, the Balkans, and Russia

It is difficult for a human being to be happy in a country...that is hostile to him. Or to be happy in an unhappy country, milieu or class. There can be no happiness at one's home if there is none in his country.

> —*Wladyslaw Tartarkiewicz*
> *"The Solidarity of Happiness"*

Martial law declared in Poland
December 13, 1981

That day
hit you in the face
if you had one.

> —*from "That Day" by Marek Baterowicz*
> *translated by Victor Contoski*

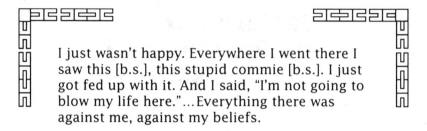

I just wasn't happy. Everywhere I went there I
saw this [b.s.], this stupid commie [b.s.]. I just
got fed up with it. And I said, "I'm not going to
blow my life here."...Everything there was
against me, against my beliefs.

> —*Slawomir Hadziewicz*
> *Political refugee from Poland, 1983*

...Perhaps we are all afraid deep down in our
hearts of losing days, hours, seconds, there is a
great impatience: something must happen.

> —*Jerzy Kepa*
> *Polish student*

People are more strongly aware of bad social
conditions than good ones. As a rule, people
think as little about a good socio-political
system as about the good air they breathe.

> —*Wladyslaw Tartarkiewicz*
> *"The Solidarity of Happiness"*

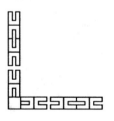

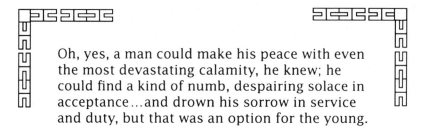

Oh, yes, a man could make his peace with even
the most devastating calamity, he knew; he
could find a kind of numb, despairing solace in
acceptance…and drown his sorrow in service
and duty, but that was an option for the young.

> —*Pan Zagloba*
> *Quoted in* With Fire and Sword
> *by Henryk Sienkiewicz*
> *(Copernicus Society of America)*

Often we complain that we are slaves to
the many things we need, to which we have
become accustomed and which we own. But
this is partly an inevitable captivity…it is
impossible to be free of everything, to give up
everything, in life, because life would then be
empty. The average person has no intention
of listening to the Stoics.

> —*Wladyslaw Tartarkiewicz*
> *"The Solidarity of Happiness"*

He is happy who wholeheartedly devotes himself to some cause, who is fully absorbed by
the reality of troubles, events, colors,
sounds…and not he who constantly sees only
himself faced by difficulties and events.

> —*Jôsef Pieter*
> *Polish psychologist*

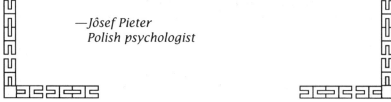

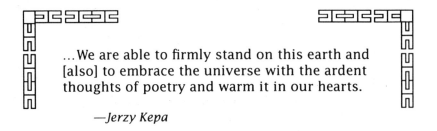

...We are able to firmly stand on this earth and [also] to embrace the universe with the ardent thoughts of poetry and warm it in our hearts.

—*Jerzy Kepa*

If all the landlords became tenants and all the tenants were landlords, everything would be just the same.

—*Polish saying*

God will repay you.

—*A Polish expression of thanks*

The giver should forget, but the receiver should remember forever.

—*Polish proverb*

Life is like the moon: now dark, now full.

—*Polish proverb*

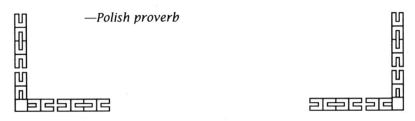

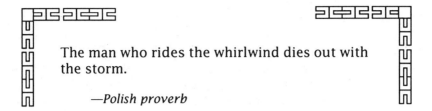

The man who rides the whirlwind dies out with the storm.

   —Polish proverb

God grant me a strong sword and no use for it.

   —Polish proverb

If there is no wind, row.

   —Polish proverb

Everything can be taken away from a man but one thing: the last of the human freedoms— to choose one's attitude in any given set of circumstances.

   —Viktor Frankl
   Holocaust survivor

We all live with the objective of being happy; our lives are all different, and yet the same.

   —Anne Frank

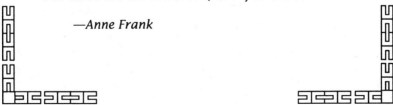

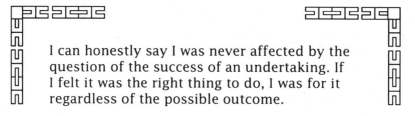

I can honestly say I was never affected by the
question of the success of an undertaking. If
I felt it was the right thing to do, I was for it
regardless of the possible outcome.

> —*Golda Meir*
> *Russian-born premier of Israel*

And if not now, when?

> —*The Talmud, collection of ancient*
> *rabbinic writings basic to Judaism*

There are three whose lives are lacking: the
over-compassionate, the hot-tempered, and the
too-squeamish.

> —*The Talmud*

Make sure to be in with your equals if you're
going to fall out with your superiors.

> —*Yiddish saying*

When you need salt, sugar won't do.

> —*Yiddish saying*

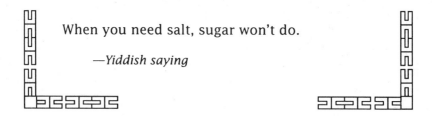

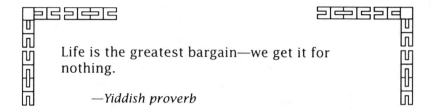

Life is the greatest bargain—we get it for nothing.

> —*Yiddish proverb*

One does not live on joy or die of sorrow.

> —*Yiddish proverb*

Only by looking outward, by caring for things that, in terms of pure survival, you needn't bother with at all...and by throwing yourself over and over again into the tumult of the world, with the intent of making your voice count—only thus will you really become a person.

> —*Vaclav Havel*
> *Playwright and first elected*
> *president of Czechoslovakia*

Right in the middle of Prague, Wenceslaus Square, there's this guy throwing up. And this other guy comes along, takes a look at him and says, "I know just what you mean."

> —*Milan Kundera*

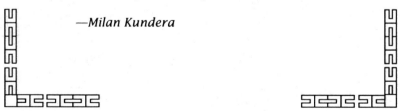

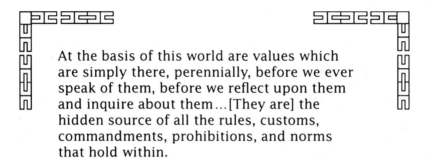

At the basis of this world are values which are simply there, perennially, before we ever speak of them, before we reflect upon them and inquire about them...[They are] the hidden source of all the rules, customs, commandments, prohibitions, and norms that hold within.

> —*Vaclav Havel*
> *"Politics and Conscience,"*
> *in* Living in Truth

Don't jump high in a low-ceilinged room.

> —*Czech proverb*

Wisdom is easy to carry but difficult to gather.

> —*Czech proverb*

The God who gave us teeth will also give us bread.

> —*Czech proverb*

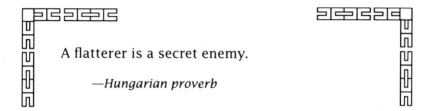

A flatterer is a secret enemy.

—*Hungarian proverb*

I have a sneaky suspicion that human beings have not really changed very much in many respects. That's a wonderful thing and a horrible thing about them. It's wonderful in the way they're so sturdy, and it's horrible because they don't learn any lessons from history. They still love violence, they still like to hurt each other. It's essentially what they were hundreds of years ago, if not thousands of years.

—*Charles Simic*
Yugoslav poet

He is not an honest man who has burned his tongue and does not tell the company the soup is hot.

—*Yugoslav proverb*

If you wish to know what a person is, place him in authority.

—*Yugoslav proverb*

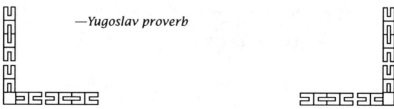

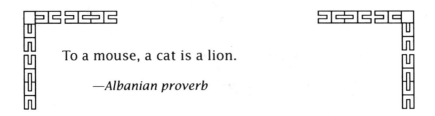

To a mouse, a cat is a lion.

—Albanian proverb

One who lies for you will also lie against you.

—Bosnian proverb

...American culture is a bit self-contained. It seems that it almost doesn't need this feeding from outside. But it's a bit dangerous. You lose your attitude [about] what's going on....In the future, America should open itself up to the rest of the world.

—Lyubomir Nikolov
Bulgarian poet now living in Pittsburgh

If you wish to drown, don't punish yourself with shallow water.

—Bulgarian proverb

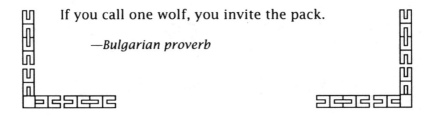

If you call one wolf, you invite the pack.

—Bulgarian proverb

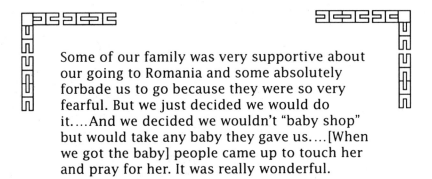

Some of our family was very supportive about our going to Romania and some absolutely forbade us to go because they were so very fearful. But we just decided we would do it....And we decided we wouldn't "baby shop" but would take any baby they gave us....[When we got the baby] people came up to touch her and pray for her. It was really wonderful.

> —*Reva Nordhagen,*
> *on adopting an abandoned baby*
> *from an orphanage in Romania*

Self-praise is no recommendation.

> —*Romanian proverb*

A tree near the road is easily felled.

> —*Serbian proverb*

Who does not thank for little will not thank for much.

> —*Estonian proverb*

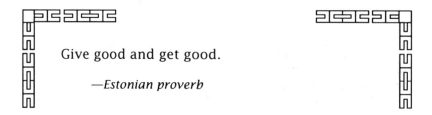

Give good and get good.

—*Estonian proverb*

The person who gives is a person who has.

—*Lithuanian proverb*

It is not without reason that Russia and the United States have drifted into a kind of collusion after their years of bitter opposition to one another, for the fact of the matter is that they have a great deal in common...not the least of these shared characteristics is size. Britain, France, and others have hacked Empires out of the available corners of the earth...but neither Britain nor France has had to come to terms with the endless horizon, mile after mile in all directions, leading to an infinity of miles....In America, the wild men, the lawless, those with a golden glimmer in the drink-sodden eye, opened up the West just as before them the shaggy cowboys called Cossacks, fugitives from justice all, opened up the East in Siberia....There it was not yet the Gold Rush, merely the Fur Rush....

—*Peter Ustinov*
Dear Me *(Penguin)*

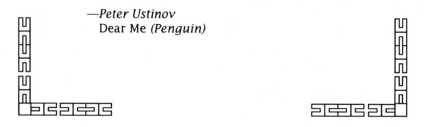

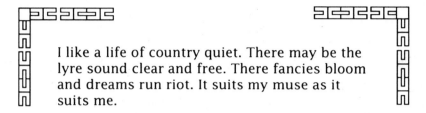

I like a life of country quiet. There may be the lyre sound clear and free. There fancies bloom and dreams run riot. It suits my muse as it suits me.

> —*Alexander Pushkin*
> Eugene Onegin

...Unhappy men are selfish, wicked, unjust, and less able to understand each other than fools. Unhappiness does not unite people but separates them.

> —*Anton Chekhov*
> Enemies

While we educated people are rummaging among old rags and, according to Russian custom, biting one another, there is boiling around us a life we neither know nor notice.

> —*Anton Chekhov*

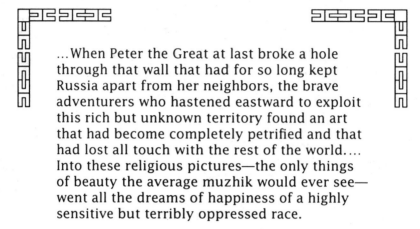

...When Peter the Great at last broke a hole
through that wall that had for so long kept
Russia apart from her neighbors, the brave
adventurers who hastened eastward to exploit
this rich but unknown territory found an art
that had become completely petrified and that
had lost all touch with the rest of the world....
Into these religious pictures—the only things
of beauty the average muzhik would ever see—
went all the dreams of happiness of a highly
sensitive but terribly oppressed race.

> —*Hendrik Willem Van Loon*
> The Arts

Two great fears dominate the creative process
in the Soviet Union: fear of official censorship,
and fear of proceeding out of ignorance of
the precise attitude the government will take
toward literature in the future. The Soviet
author is not only harassed, he is harassed
for reasons which have not been properly
explained to him and which seem to change
constantly and capriciously.

> —*Donald W. Heiney*
> Essentials of Contemporary Literature

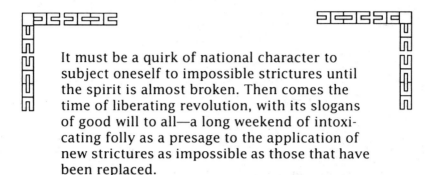

It must be a quirk of national character to subject oneself to impossible strictures until the spirit is almost broken. Then comes the time of liberating revolution, with its slogans of good will to all—a long weekend of intoxicating folly as a presage to the application of new strictures as impossible as those that have been replaced.

> —*Peter Ustinov*
> Dear Me

The little one is too small; the big one is too big; the medium one is just right—but I can't reach it.

> —*Russian Proverb*

Fear life, not death.

> —*Russian proverb*

Mosquitoes sing over the living, priests over the dead.

> —*Russian proverb*

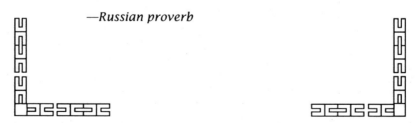

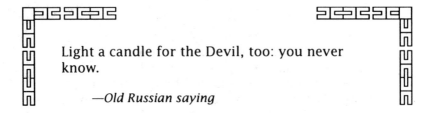

Light a candle for the Devil, too: you never know.

—*Old Russian saying*

When money speaks, truth keeps quiet.

—*Russian proverb*

Death does not take the old but the ripe.

—*Russian proverb*

Don't worry if you borrow—worry if you lend.

—*Russian proverb*

A kind word is like a Spring day.

—*Russian proverb*

India, the Middle East, and North Africa

In matters of conscience, the law of majority has no place.

—*(Mohandas K.) Mahatma Gandhi (1869–1948)*
Hindu nationalist and spiritual leader

I think it would be a good idea.

—*Mahatma Gandhi, when asked what he*
thought of Western civilization

There is more to life than increasing its speed.

—*Mahatma Gandhi*

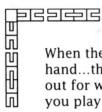

When the cards are dealt and you pick up your hand...there's nothing you can do except play it out for whatever it may be worth. And the way you play your hand is free will.

> —*Jawaharlal Nehru (1889–1964)*
> *First Prime Minister of India*

Government is the science of punishment.

> —*The* Arthashastra, *a manual for*
> *heads of state c. 260 B.C.*

All sects deserve reverence for one reason or another. By thus acting a man exalts his own sect and at the same time does service to the sects of other people.

> —*Emperor Ashoka, 2nd century B.C.*

He who allows his day to pass without practicing generosity and enjoying life's pleasures is like a blacksmith's bellows—he breathes but does not live.

> —*Sanskrit proverb*

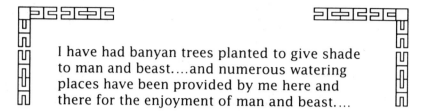

I have had banyan trees planted to give shade
to man and beast....and numerous watering
places have been provided by me here and
there for the enjoyment of man and beast....

Formerly in the kitchen of his Sacred and
Gracious Majesty, many hundreds of thousands
of living creatures were slaughtered every day
to make curries. But now...only three living
creatures are slaughtered for curry, to wit, two
peacocks and an antelope—the antelope, however, not invariably.

*—from proclamations of Emperor Ashoka
to teach the doctrine of "ahimsa,"
or non-violence, and the sacredness
of all living things*

Strenuousness is the open foe of attainment.
The strength that wins is calm and has an
exhaustless source in its passive depth.

*—Sir Rabindranath Tagore (1861–1941)
Indian poet*

Change comes as an enemy only to those who
have lost the art of accepting it as a friend.

—Rabindranath Tagore

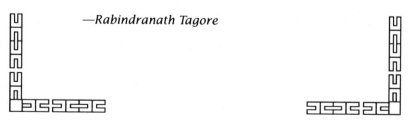

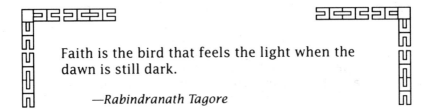

Faith is the bird that feels the light when the dawn is still dark.

—*Rabindranath Tagore*

Like the body that is made up of different limbs and organs, all mortal creatures exist depending upon one another.

—*Hindu proverb*

When an elephant is in trouble, even a frog will kick him.

—*Hindu proverb*

He who cannot dance puts the blame on the floor.

—*Hindu proverb*

Call on God, but row away from the rocks.

—*Indian proverb*

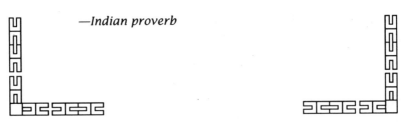

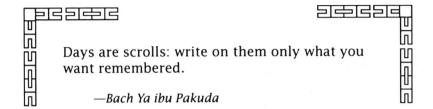

Days are scrolls: write on them only what you want remembered.

—*Bach Ya ibu Pakuda*

Avoid friends and followers who are detrimental to thy peace of mind.

—*Tibetan Rosary of Precious Gems*

If I had but two loaves of bread, I would sell one and buy hyacinths, for they would feed my soul.

—*The Koran*

The Moving Finger writes; and having writ,
Moves on; nor all your Piety nor Wit
   Shall lure it back to cancel half a Line,
Nor all your Tears wash out a Word of it.

—*from the* Rubiayat *of Omar Khayyam
(11th century Persian, translated by
Edward Fitzgerald)*

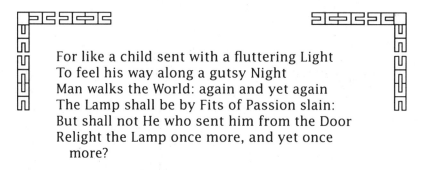

For like a child sent with a fluttering Light
To feel his way along a gutsy Night
Man walks the World: again and yet again
The Lamp shall be by Fits of Passion slain:
But shall not He who sent him from the Door
Relight the Lamp once more, and yet once
     more?

> —*from the* Mantik-ut-tair *or*
> Parliament of Birds *by Attar*
> *(Translated from the Persian[1] by Edward*
> *Fitzgerald)*

Who possesses much silver may be happy;
who possesses much barley may be glad;
but he who has nothing may sleep.

> —*Saying from Mesopotamia*[2]

If you take the field of an enemy,
the enemy will come and take your field.

> —*Mesopotamian proverb*

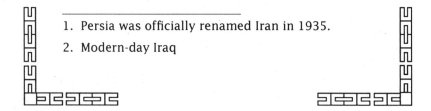

1. Persia was officially renamed Iran in 1935.

2. Modern-day Iraq

Some of you say, "Joy is greater than
sorrow," and others say, "Nay, sorrow is
the greater."
 But I say unto you, they are inseparable.
 Together they come, and when one sits alone
with you at your board, remember that the
other is asleep upon your bed.

> —*from* The Prophet
> *by Kahlil Gibran, Lebanese poet (1883–1931)*

Fear the person who fears you.

> —*Middle Eastern proverb*

A miser is like a person with bread who is
starving.

> —*Middle Eastern proverb*

When you shoot an arrow of truth, dip its point
in honey.

> —*Arab proverb*

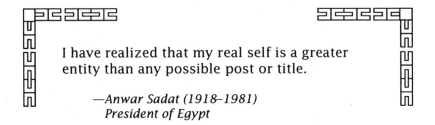

I have realized that my real self is a greater entity than any possible post or title.

—Anwar Sadat (1918–1981)
President of Egypt

Health is a crown on a well man's head, but no one can see it but a sick man.

—A wise Egyptian

He who fears something gives it power over him.

—Moorish proverb

In the eyes of its mother, every beetle is a gazelle.

—Moroccan proverb

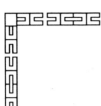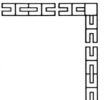

Asia and Asian America

Ignorance is the night of the mind, but a night without moon or star.

—*Confucius*
Chinese philosopher and teacher

To be wronged is nothing unless you continue to remember it.

—*Confucius*

Notice the natural order of things. Work with it rather than against it for to try to change what is so will only set up resistance.

—*Lao Tzu, book of Taoist teaching*

I observe myself and so I come to know others.

—*Lao Tzu*

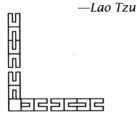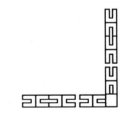

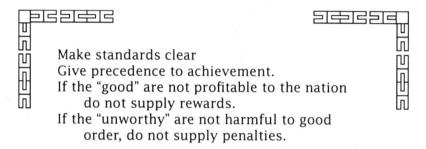

Make standards clear
Give precedence to achievement.
If the "good" are not profitable to the nation
    do not supply rewards.
If the "unworthy" are not harmful to good
    order, do not supply penalties.

—*W'ang Ch'ung*
Philosopher

We think too small. Like the frog at the bottom
of the well. He thinks the sky is only as big as
the top of the well. If he surfaced, he would
have an entirely different view.

—*Mao-Tse-Tung*

For is it not true that human progress is but a
mighty growing pattern woven together by the
tenuous single threads united in a common
effort?

—*Soong Mei-ling*
(Madame Chiang-Kai-shek)

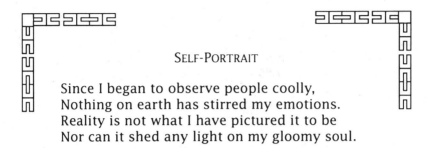

SELF-PORTRAIT

Since I began to observe people coolly,
Nothing on earth has stirred my emotions.
Reality is not what I have pictured it to be
Nor can it shed any light on my gloomy soul.

When I summed up the experiences of life
    I gradually lost my poetic innocence.
For a society in which black is called white
I no longer have a light heart to play my fiddle.

      —Poster from the Xidan Democracy Wall
        China, 1979

Everyone is born destined to seek freedom.
Wouldn't anyone enjoy freedom and leisure
and the pleasure of doing what he likes? To
enjoy freedom and do what one likes are basic
freedoms....There will never be a time when
human beings voluntarily turn down opportu-
nities to do their own thinking and manage
their own lives.

      —Poster from the Xidan Democracy Wall
        China, 1979

Sweep away last year's dust and all bad
feelings.

      —Chinese New Year saying

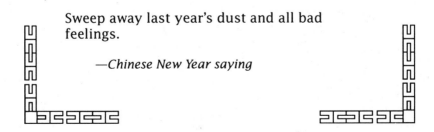

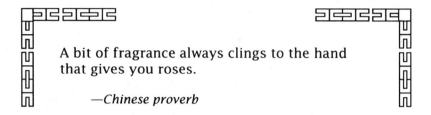

A bit of fragrance always clings to the hand that gives you roses.

—*Chinese proverb*

The beginning of wisdom is to call things by their right names.

—*Chinese proverb*

A man who has to be punctually at a certain place at five o'clock has the whole afternoon ruined for him already.

—*Lin Yutang*
The Importance of Living *(John Day)*

On example: Not the cry but the flight of the wild duck, leads the flock to fly and follow.

—*Chinese proverb*

The nail that sticks up gets hammered down.

—*Chinese saying*

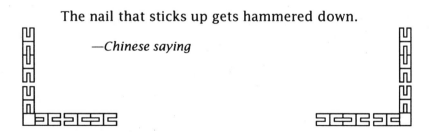

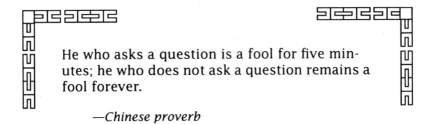

He who asks a question is a fool for five min-
utes; he who does not ask a question remains a
fool forever.

—Chinese proverb

A whitewashed cow will not remain white long.

—Chinese proverb

Patience is power; with time and patience the
mulberry leaf becomes a silk gown.

—Chinese proverb

Those who have free seats at the play hiss first.

—Chinese proverb

It is the beautiful bird which gets caged.

—Chinese proverb

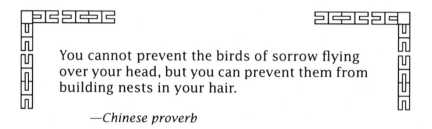

You cannot prevent the birds of sorrow flying over your head, but you can prevent them from building nests in your hair.

—*Chinese proverb*

A good teacher is like a reservoir behind a dam....[he or she] must continually educate himself to be able to supply the knowledge that students need. A good teacher needs both a scholastic mind and compassion.

—*Yoshiaki Takahashi*
Teacher of English in Tokyo

You should not have your own idea when you listen to someone....To have nothing in your mind is naturalness. Then you will understand what he says.

—*Shunryu Suzuki*

To receive a favor is to sell one's liberty.

—*Japanese proverb*

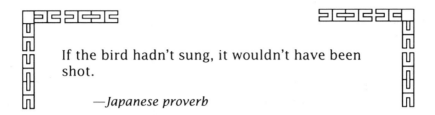

If the bird hadn't sung, it wouldn't have been shot.

> —*Japanese proverb*

To an ant a few drops of rain is a flood.

> —*Japanese proverb*

A turtle travels only when it sticks its neck out.

> —*Korean proverb*

Even a fish wouldn't get into trouble if it kept its mouth shut.

> —*Korean proverb*

Give an extra piece of cake to a stepchild.

> —*Korean proverb*

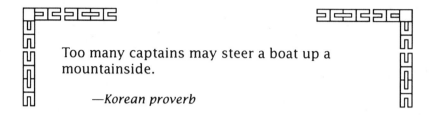

Too many captains may steer a boat up a mountainside.

—*Korean proverb*

Sometimes we think we have to express our feelings in order to feel better. But you don't have to keep touching your suffering a lot. You should have reserves of refreshing images to counterbalance the suffering within you.

—*Thich Nahat Hanh*

Don't borrow another's nose to breathe with.

—*Thai proverb*

Cultivate a heart of love that knows no anger.

—*Cambodian proverb*

Live with vultures, become a vulture; live with crows, become a crow.

—*Laotian proverb*

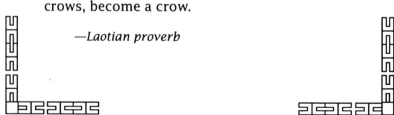

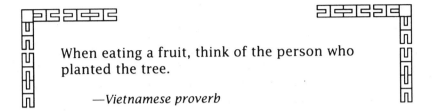

When eating a fruit, think of the person who planted the tree.

       —Vietnamese proverb

On differences: Sun is good for cucumbers, rain for rice.

       —Vietnamese proverb

Nice words are free, so choose ones to please another's ears.

       —Vietnamese proverb

"I loved my country and didn't want to leave my motherland, because my ancestors are buried there and also because I had to leave my brothers and sisters behind. But living conditions under communism became impossible, and I don't think the communists will go away there like they have in other countries..."

       —Le Xua
       Vietnamese immigrant

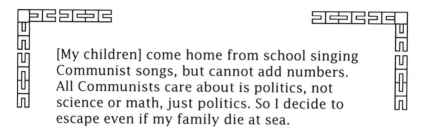

[My children] come home from school singing
Communist songs, but cannot add numbers.
All Communists care about is politics, not
science or math, just politics. So I decide to
escape even if my family die at sea.

> —*Nguyen Huu Gi*
> *Computer store owner,*
> *formerly a math teacher in Vietnam*

Americans go to bank for loan, Vietnamese
go to friends. I ask this guy for a thousand,
another for two thousand, soon I have eighteen
thousand. We trust each other, so no interest.
He know I do the same for him one day.

> —*Nguyen Huu Gi*

I'm too old to start again. The future belongs to
my children. That is why we are here.

> —*"Lihn"*
> *Former South Vietnamese Air Force major*

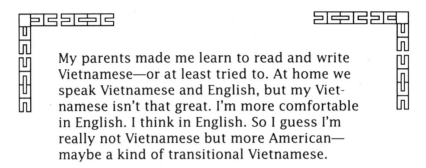

My parents made me learn to read and write Vietnamese—or at least tried to. At home we speak Vietnamese and English, but my Vietnamese isn't that great. I'm more comfortable in English. I think in English. So I guess I'm really not Vietnamese but more American—maybe a kind of transitional Vietnamese.

> *—Kieu Oanh Nguyen Ha*
> *Student, Advanced Placement English*
> *Saddleback High School, California*

I feel shackled in Little Saigon [the Vietnamese community in Orange County, California]. When I grow up, I want to live in some place like Maine, where it's not all Vietnamese, and I can play bridge with my neighbors on Thursday night.

> *—Minh Le Tran*
> *Student, Advanced Placement English*
> *Saddleback High School, California*